★ A SURVIVAL GUIDE FOR ★

LIFE IN THE PUBLIC ARENA

Sam Reed

Secretary of State, 2001-2013

To Margie,

*my toughest critic
and most loyal supporter.*

Sam and Margie, Summer 2000.

CONTENTS

Sam in front of a Capitol pillar in 2011

Preface

AS I CONCLUDE MY 45 YEARS of public service, I am asked not only how I survived this long in the rough-and-tumble field of politics but also obviously continue to find it interesting, rewarding and fun.

I was a deeply fortunate young man. When I arrived in Olympia in 1967 to work in state government, I was surrounded with political giants who had a profound, lasting influence on my view of public service and my conduct as a public official.

Governor Dan Evans, State Representative and future Congressman Joel Pritchard, and Evans' chief of staff and future state Supreme Court Chief Justice Jim Dolliver taught me about civility, moderation and bipartisanship. They conveyed a deep respect for the political craft. By example, I learned the key to success is surrounding one's self with bright, articulate, innovative, caring, talented staff members. Participating in the Governor's Two-Mile Run and having extensive contact with the Evans family taught me the importance of taking care of yourself and your family.

As I conclude my career, I want to share these lessons with future political generations. I have loved my years in the political arena, and I have thrived. In my 10 years of working for other elected officials and 35 years as a county-elected, then state-elected official, I've worked with hundreds of others elected to office. I've seen some self-destruct, some burn out, and others just get by and fade away. I've also observed those who have flourished throughout their political careers.

The question is, how does one continue to flourish?

In this modest little handbook, I am attempting to explain how one can have a lifetime career in politics and thrive.

I talk about leadership, political craftsmanship, how to work with one's staff, and the critically important personal aspects of a public life.

It is my hope that some of the insights I've learned will be as helpful to others as those of Governor Evans, Justice Dolliver and Congressman Pritchard helped my generation.

Sam Reed

1

POLITICAL LEADERSHIP:

Help them realize how exceptional they are.

The Secrets of America's Great Presidents: *"Courage to stay strong; self-confidence; ability to learn from errors; willingness to change; emotional intelligence; the popular touch; a moral compass; a capacity to relax, and a gift for inspiring others."*

—Doris Kearns Goodwin

ONE OF THE DIVIDENDS of serving in state and county government for 45 years was the opportunity to observe seven Governors, seven U.S. Senators, many U.S. House members, a host of statewide elected officials, legislators and local government officials. Call me weird, but I truly like and respect politicians. A few strike me as exceptional when it comes to vision and inspiration. I'll explain.

As a young tiger, fresh out of Washington State University's Graduate School of Political Science, I arrived in Olympia to work for Washington's legendary Governor Dan Evans. The moderate, pragmatic Republican served an unprecedented three consecutive terms. We staffers would have walked through fire for him. Why? Because Evans had all those crucial gifts identified above by author Doris Kearns Goodwin, chief among them, the ability to inspire others.

As with many other young Evans staffers who went on to a career in public service, I was deeply inspired by his vision for our state's future and the forward-looking, cutting-edge public policies he fearlessly championed. I discovered the amazing power created when people are fired up and working together for a worthy, challenging goal. You get that gut feeling that you're making a difference—even, perhaps, making history.

Governor Evans didn't believe in holding a finger to the wind or basing policy on polls. He envisioned what the state should look like in the future and based his policy initiatives on that. We staffers felt as if we were helping to build a legacy beyond ourselves, and we gave our all because we believed in what we were doing. We experienced the exhilaration of doing something important and contributing to moving our communities and state forward.

From my experience in the late 1960s and '70s, I came to realize it was important to focus my time and energy on making a difference. That helped me set priorities.

I have vivid memories of the lessons in political courage I learned from Dan Evans. One case especially resonates with me: I was responsible for promoting a highly controversial executive-request bill. After heated meetings with state senators, I told the governor he would pay a steep political price if we kept pushing the bill and advised it would be politically wise to back off. Evans asked me only one question: "Is it (the proposal) the *right* thing to do?" I said it clearly was. "Then," he said, "We are going to get this bill through." Rather than hoarding his political capital, he was willing to risk it to achieve a worthy goal. The bill passed.

In the short run, Governor Evans paid a stiff political price. But—and this was my lesson—in the long run, it turned out to be politically beneficial because it was the right thing to do for the state. Evans taught us that political timidity rarely solved important problems. In those early years in my career,

I learned that inspiration and vision are the core of extraordinary leadership.

Three decades later, I learned some tough lessons during the 2004 Gregoire-Rossi governor's race, the most controversial election in Washington's history. The lessons revolved around integrity and transparency.

During the election recounts, I was reproached by both parties. The Democrats were sure the (pick an expletive) Republican Secretary of State was working overtime, down and dirty, to elect the GOP's Dino Rossi by not complying with their proposed changes in the recount. The Republicans were sure that if I only had some backbone I could change what was happening when the lead switched to the Democrats' Christine Gregoire. I weathered blistering attacks on talk radio and in the blogs. Even some long-time political friends and allies were angry with me for not "doing something" or for positions I took on recount procedures and legal briefs for court cases.

In the midst of all that rancor and relentless stress, people asked me if I was able to sleep at night. My answer was always, "Yes. No problem," which was the truth. After conducting dozens of recounts—including two hotly contested congressional races—while serving as Thurston County Auditor, I knew exactly what to do. Moreover, I was doing the right thing: complying with my oath to uphold the constitution and laws of the state of Washington. And while I was angry with King County for major mistakes and a lack of openness (and used my bully pulpit to say so), I also understood it was King County Executive Ron Sims, not the Secretary of State, who had authority over the county's elections operations.

Despite both political parties' sharp criticism, I emerged politically stronger than before. The public appreciated the fact that I didn't play political games and didn't put my finger on the scale. They viewed me as conducting the recounts with integrity, as doing the right thing. The lesson is that credibility—the public trust—is crucial to success in the public arena.

Throughout the years, I've observed that personal integrity and high ethical standards are nonnegotiable. In his first inaugural address as the youngest governor in state history, Dan Evans said, "I'd rather cross the aisle than cross the people."

But integrity is not enough. Transparency also is critically important. In the 2000 presidential election recount, Florida's Secretary of State, Katherine Harris, adopted a bunker mentality. She hid out in a guarded room and communicated with the press only through announcements. Questions were not permitted. In terms of public trust and confidence, it was an unmitigated disaster.

Mindful of the Florida fiasco, I overcompensated during the 2004 gubernatorial recount. At the press conference calling for a recount, I gallantly proclaimed, "Any time any of you have any questions, call me!" It didn't occur to me that my home phone number was listed. Calls hounded me from early in the morning until late at night seven days a week. One talk-radio station couldn't resist calling without warning at 6:05 a.m. and, as I blinked myself awake, putting me on live regarding the latest controversy. While my "any time" vow was excessive, I believe the people of the state of Washington had the right to know what was happening and why. It was their election.

The importance of transparency also applies to mistakes and problems. Looking back on Watergate, President Richard Nixon conceded that a cover-up was the biggest blunder a politician could make. If he had admitted early on to the American people that the break-in at Democratic headquarters was a terrible error, the "cancer growing on the presidency" likely would never have metastasized. The lesson here is that if you or your agency goof up, be the one who announces the problem to the public. The truth may not always set you free but it is far preferable to denial or obfuscation. In the short run, you take negative hits (I have—and it isn't any fun), but in the long run, your honesty with the public you serve stands to gain their trust and confidence. It is the right thing.

> The Qualities of a Successful Political Leader:
> *"Self-confidence; curiosity; an eye for talent;*
> *the ability to communicate, and the temperament*
> *that invites collaboration."*
>
> —David Broder, late dean of the U. S. Capitol Press Corps

While I don't consider myself the most brilliant or talented person around, I have one particularly strong quality: an eye for talent. I have been exceptionally successful at surrounding myself with outstanding people, recruiting them to my staff and my volunteer activities. I have built teams that had fun while pulling off substantial accomplishments.

What are the secrets to success? They're simple.

First, I'm not afraid to recruit the smartest, most capable people I can find. Some leaders feel threatened by people who are smarter or more talented than they are. I am just the opposite. I love to be surrounded by creative, confident people. Giving them the opportunity to make a difference is enormously gratifying to me.

Second, I have the audacity to ask. Some leaders make the mistake of assuming that an exceptionally capable person wouldn't come to work for them or volunteer for their cause. However, the worst they can say is "no," so I ask. Of course, it's not really that simple. You need to do your homework. Learn what pushes that person's buttons. Explain why your cause should be his or her cause. Tell them why they can make a difference if they come to work with you. U.S. Senators Warren G. Magnuson and Slade Gorton took enormous pride in the exceptional young men and women they hired. Long after they left office, they were still making a difference through the people they had gathered around them. They left a legacy.

A quote I've always kept on my desk summarizes my idea of leadership. It says: "The goal of most leaders it to get the people to think highly of the leader. But the goal of the exceptional leader is to get the people to think highly of themselves." In other words, rather than spending your time trying to impress your staff or team, spend your time helping them realize how exceptional they are.

So, that's it. During my 45 years in public service, I found the keys to successful leadership. They are vision, inspiration, integrity, transparency and surrounding yourself with great people. This is as true in the private sector and in volunteer activities as it is in government. The secrets really aren't secrets. You can do it too, whether you aspire to be president of your local bank, the Kiwanis Club or the United States.

2

POLITICAL CRAFTSMANSHIP:
We need civility, moderation and bipartisanship.

"It is not the critic who counts; not the man who points
out how the strong man stumbled, or where the doer of
deeds could have done better. The credit belongs to the
man who is actually in the arena; whose face is marred
by dust and sweat and blood; who strives valiantly; who
errs and comes up short again and again; who knows
the great enthusiasms, the great devotions, and spends
himself in a worthy cause; who at the best knows in the
end the triumph of high achievement; and who at the
worst, if he fails, at least fails while daring greatly; so that
his place shall never be with those cold and timid souls
who know neither victory or defeat."

—Theodore Roosevelt

WHEN I WAS A KID IN WENATCHEE, my grandfather Sam Sumner, for whom I am named, inspired, entertained, educated and conveyed the profound importance of history to his grandchildren. One message permanently implanted in my brain was this, "Politics is the highest calling."

Sam Sumner was a former State Representative, prosecuting attorney and Washington State Republican Party chairman. He also was a Lincoln scholar and a lifelong student of the U.S. Constitution. Sunday dinner with my grandfather always featured a captivating history lesson on politics and history. He always said it was vital to respect the institution and all its components. It is little wonder that I not only made a career of politics, but also have done so with great respect for public service.

When Ryne Sandberg, the Spokane native who starred at second base for the Chicago Cubs, was inducted into the Baseball Hall of Fame, this is what he said: "The reason I am here, they tell me, is that I played the game a certain way; that I played the game the way it was supposed to be played. I don't know about that, but I do know this: I had too much respect for the game to play it any other way, and if there was a single reason I am here today, it is because of one word: respect. I love to play baseball. I'm a baseball player. I've always been

a baseball player. I'm still a baseball player. That's who I am."
I'm a political Ryne Sandberg. I'm proud to be a politician.
I have found great joy in politics. I believe in playing the game
the way it is supposed to be played—with civility, moderation,
bipartisanship, respect for other players, attention to ceremony
and protocols, and a commitment to continued learning from
current and historical political figures.

In our state, we had a politically disastrous example of the
opposite viewpoint: Governor Dixy Lee Ray. A first-rate scientist
and compelling professor, she nevertheless took pride in
not being a politician, as if the profession was worthy only of
contempt and little more than a sinecure for hacks, ward heelers
and grafters. She viewed the other players and the political
process with icy disdain. She let the Capitol Press Corps know
what she thought of it by naming the pigs on her farm after her
least favorite reporters. She ridiculed the Legislature. She even
disrespected such political giants as Dan Evans and Warren
Magnuson. As a consequence, by consensus, she joined Roland
Hartley as one of the two worst, most ineffective Governors
in our state's history. As soon as Washington citizens had a
chance, they voted her out of office by a landslide—in the primary
election, no less.

In starkest contrast is Joel Pritchard, a moderate Republican who served in both the Washington House of Representatives and Senate and in the U.S. House of Representatives, as well as being our state's Lieutenant Governor. He was a consummate politician in the finest sense of the word, a bipartisan practitioner of the politics of the possible.

Joel's sayings are legendary around the State Capitol. One sums up Dixy Lee Ray's problem: "Some people are all propeller and no rudder."

Pritchard served as a mentor and role model for my political generation. He was an exemplar of civility and bipartisanship throughout his career, having had remarkable success in Congress working across the aisle. He emphasized to us the importance of "doing your chores," meaning making the time to return phone calls; sending hand-written notes of thanks and encouragement; engaging people in their communities; and mentoring the next political generation. He stressed respect for the other players in the political process—constituents, other politicians, the media and lobbyists. Describing effective legislators, Joel said, "They know how to work in a bipartisan fashion on most issues and respect the sincerity of those who oppose their point of view. The effective legislator, like an effective person in any field, is able to discuss issues without personal rancor."

Another of Joel's memorable principles was: "It's amazing what you can accomplish if you do not care who gets credit."

He exemplified the traits of a strong leader, one who effectively communicates with others, builds strong political relationships, and treats opponents with civility.

Something I've noticed over the years is that the best public officeholders are motivated by a heartfelt conviction that they can and will make a valuable contribution. They don't view the office as "just a job," a vehicle for getting a pension or a stepping stone to a higher elected office. I can assure you that the public can tell the difference. If you're seeking office, and the people put their trust in you, my advice is this: Don't just fill the office. Make history. Colleagues and staff members will recognize your commitment—and help you make a difference. Without it, we all suffer, and we lose opportunities for excellence. Leaders need to build a legacy beyond themselves. Politics should be animated by exciting, challenging ideas.

If you *lack* the right motivation, don't run for office. I learned that lesson the hard way. When the Thurston County commissioners helped defeat an excellent Home Rule Charter, I was upset and ran against one of them, planning to reintroduce the charter process. I managed to grab defeat from the jaws of victory in the midst of a Republican landslide. What happened? Voters could sense I really didn't want to be a County Commissioner. The worst officeholders are those who run because the office provides a political opportunity rather than because they care deeply about what can be accomplished in the position. Champion your causes, but make sure they're about more than just you.

To accomplish anything of consequence, help people understand why your idea matters. Too many officeholders won't risk their stature by making themselves vulnerable to criticism from the news media, using up their political capital or risking failure. Success is achieved by doing the opposite. You need to build your relationship with the media by getting out there and fighting for your causes. You expand your political capital by using your political chits to advocate issues—win, lose or draw. If you fall short, you simply learn how to do it better next time. Looking back over my 45 years in politics, I certainly can attest to that. I failed in my attempts to get a state constitutional convention. I failed in my campaign for state auditor. But those experiences taught me a great deal. I established a statewide network of political allies and learned from my mistakes, setting the groundwork for my three successful campaigns for secretary of state.

Partially because of those learning experiences, I have not hesitated to vigorously advocate for my causes by meeting with newspaper editorial boards, participating in radio and television interviews and forums, giving speeches to service clubs and contacting key public officials and other opinion leaders.

To further those causes, I have learned, you must be well-prepared with compelling arguments, key facts, cogent talking points (not platitudes) and informative handouts that people actually can and will read. It's important to do your homework and know your audience so you can be prepared to make points that resonate with them.

Public speaking is at or near the top of every list of people's worst fears. To be an effective politician—or any sort of leader—you must learn to overcome that phobia. Getting involved in service clubs, Toastmasters or leadership of other volunteer activities is a good way to start. The more talks you give and the more preparation and practice you do, the better you become. Honing public speaking skills is crucial, as is becoming familiar with all media platforms. Reaching out to a television audience is far different from giving a Rotary Club talk.

Undergirding these efforts are creating effective partnerships and long-term alliances. It is important to build relationships with bright, motivated people who will support you in worthy causes. And it is important to maintain these allies through phone calls, notes, e-mail updates and other social media. As with friendship or marriage, you need to build and nurture these relationships. Don't wait until you need their help.

Keeping focused also is fundamental to success. Know your goal and develop a smart, effective strategy for reaching it, then persevere. Significant changes often can't be accomplished in your first attempt. While it's difficult to be patient, realize you're in for the long haul. As I wrote that sentence, my mind instantly jumped to an issue that dogged me through my entire 12 years as Secretary of State: our primary election system.

When California appropriated our time-honored blanket primary system—which lets voters vote for whomever they choose, regardless of party—many of us grew concerned. Sure enough, the California political parties sued and the U.S. Supreme Court ruled it unconstitutional. Lucky me: During my first day as Secretary of State, I was served papers for a lawsuit, *Democratic Party, et al, v. Sam Reed*. The *et al* was the Republican Party and the Libertarian Party. On that memorable day and throughout the next 10 years, friends, political allies and experts advised me to give in and give up fighting for a wide-open primary for our state.

After getting the "Top 2" Primary passed by the Legislature, adopted overwhelmingly by the people via initiative and approved 7-to-2 by the U.S. Supreme Court, we finally prevailed. While many party leaders got angry at me and others just grew weary of the fight during that process, I believed it was important to stand up for the people of the state. This primary fits our political heritage.

Another example of decisiveness and perseverance was saving our historic Washington State Library. When Governor Gary Locke announced that he planned to save money by closing one of his agencies, the State Library, I spoke out in opposition. A couple legislators heard the call to action and introduced legislation to save the library by placing it in the

Office of Secretary of State. This put me in direct opposition to the governor. My side succeeded. The library community around the state is eternally grateful for a political champion who fights for them.

These are examples of championing your cause. While these causes were challenging and involved using up many political chits, I leave office feeling they are my lasting legacy. In other words, it was worth it. Here's the bottom line in my book: If you are not ready to fight for your causes, you shouldn't be in public office. Nobody says public service is easy, even when you have "right" on your side.

On the other hand, too many doctrinaire, dogmatic, "my way or the highway" people are clogging the engine of democracy. Bipartisan politics is like civility. It requires us to consider the notion that the other guy just might be right. When I first came to Olympia and became involved in the legislative process, I was impressed by how the Republicans and Democrats could argue passionately on the floor of the Senate and House, then go out, have a drink together and socialize. Despite some strong partisan disagreements, they were able to maintain personal friendships and chat amiably about their families, their jobs, sports and life.

Unfortunately, we've lost that. Working across the aisle invariably achieves better legislation, legislation that can stand the test of time. If one party just jams the other party on a major policy issue, it likely will be reversed when the other party becomes a majority. I've observed that some of our most enduring legislation is sponsored by the moderates of both parties. They have found a way to build relationships of trust and respect across the aisle. Rather than abetting polarization, they are able to work out practical compromises and get something done.

Don't get me wrong. I'm not against political parties. I am a proud member of the party of Lincoln, but I count many Democrats as friends and allies. I believe the parties play an important role in American politics. They provide opportunities for like-minded people to work together to advance their parties' principles and policy positions. The political party organizations and their congressional and legislative caucuses also carry out the important function of recruiting and supporting quality candidates capable of winning public office and serving us well. Finally, they provide a useful cue to voters who are choosing their officeholders. Any party worth belonging to stands on core principles. But narrow partisan politics is an anathema to the public in the state of Washington and across the nation. Being strident induces cynicism and alienates potential supporters and voters.

> "Today's adversary may be tomorrow's ally."
> — Rudolph Giuliani

In politics, it is important to understand that just because a politician may be against you on an issue doesn't mean she or he is a political enemy. Former Republican State Representative Jim Clements comes to mind as a dramatic example. He was negative about many of my electoral reform proposals and furious with me over the 2004 gubernatorial election recount. I could easily have viewed him as a political enemy. However, when Governor Gary Locke proposed to eliminate the Washington State Library and I stepped up to save it, Clements shared my conviction and became my strongest, most loyal ally. We fought for the State Library shoulder-to-shoulder and succeeded.

While I always campaigned hard to win my election contests, I also made sure to treat my opponent with dignity and respect. Interestingly, most of my opponents responded by turning around and supporting me in subsequent elections! Joel Pritchard experienced that, as well. So my advice to aspiring politicians is this: Don't be a Richard Nixon with an "enemies list." Just look where that got him. Disagree agreeably and build relationships for the future, when you can agree and work together.

Perhaps most important of all, don't lose touch with the people who put you in office. It's a huge mistake to view campaigns as the only time in the political process you should be in contact with the people. Once elected, make those contacts regularly, not just every four years.

As a statewide elected official, I believe it is important to be *statewide*. Consequently, I have taken pains to keep my commitment to be present regularly in all 39 counties. And when I'm there, I don't just visit local public officials and news media. I always meet with community leaders and supporters, usually for breakfast or lunch. In medium and large counties, I have ongoing advisory committees. I share what's going on in my office and emphasize that I want to know what's happening in their communities. These gatherings are informal. We have fun. The meetings are informative for the participants and for me. It's a terrific way to stay in touch.

When speaking to clubs and forums, or just talking with three or four people over coffee, a canned pitch or speech is totally inappropriate. The concerns of folks in the Tri-Cities differ from those in Tacoma. Use your local contacts and, if possible, staff support to tailor your approach and remarks. Failure to do your homework can make you sound out of touch or, worse yet, silly. As you approach different communities, don't simply go to the population centers and speak to large gatherings. Small communities and small organizations deserve and deeply appreciate your attention. You may be the only elected official who has ever bothered to tell them they matter.

When in these communities, your most valuable contacts are your supporters. They are crucial to your long-term success. The most critical component of political craftsmanship is the recruitment and maintenance of a broad cross-section of political supporters. Without them, you can't get elected. Their help also is crucial to get something accomplished once you're in office.

In the Leadership chapter, I talked about how to recruit

volunteers. But once you have recruited them, how do you retain them? The three key components I use are appreciation, communication and loyalty.

First, express your appreciation. These are the chores that Joel Pritchard talked about. Never be too busy to send thank-you notes. While I may be a bit extreme, I always committed many hours to writing them. No carbon-copy thank-yous for me. In some cases, I added personal notes to my fundraising letters. Some people over the years have wondered why I spend so much time writing notes of appreciation, but I believe when people give their time, talent and treasure to help me get elected, they deserve a personal touch. Everyone likes being acknowledged and appreciated.

Second, have regular contact. In this era of social media, it is not difficult. From my office, I am on Facebook, Twitter, YouTube, e-mail and, previously, MySpace. My office also has a daily blog. From home, I regularly stay in touch with thousands of supporters via e-mail. I share articles, editorials and blogs about what we're doing in my office. I also write a brief personal note. When individual supporters reply, I personally respond. This again takes a considerable amount of time, but I view it as fundamental to serving in public office. By being conscientious about maintaining contact, I have retained some wonderful political friends and allies throughout my career. They have continued to be there for me, as I am for them.

Third, "dance with the one who brung you." If you want your supporters to be loyal to you, you must be loyal to them. It works both ways. Loyal supporters are more important than a politician's relationship with his or her political party, the media, other elected officials and/or lobbyists.

Everything that matters is premised on the way you conduct yourself as a person. To be a successful practitioner of political craftsmanship, certain personal qualities are crucial.

Remain humble. Too many politicians let the flattery of lobbyists and campaign supporters go to their heads. Keeping perspective is important. Lobbyists are paid to sweet-talk political leaders. Campaign supporters are advocating for you, so of course, they are going to be flattering. If you become arrogant, voters see it quickly. Political fame also is fleeting. You are playing a role in a complicated, multi-layered political process. As soon as you leave office, you face the stark reality that it was the *position*, not you, that is important.

When I became Secretary of State, I wanted the staff I inherited to know I did not suffer from an exaggerated sense of self-importance. It helped that I brought over a very clever young woman from my previous office to be my receptionist. As she had done before, Alex made me the object of witty wisecracks, quips, teasing and practical jokes. She had a deft touch, and it never crossed the line. She immediately was the hit of the office. In fact, the carryover employees selected her "Employee of the Quarter" during her first few months there. By bringing her into the office, I succeeded in showing that I'm not one of those stuffy officeholders who is "above it all" and believes "rank has its privileges." It set a tone in the office of having fun.

Speaking of puffery, some of my colleagues in the National Association of Secretaries of State insist that the public, the media and their staff members refer to them as "Mr. Secretary" or "Secretary Smith." I've seen the same around Olympia where it's always Senator this and Senator that. Oh, mercy! Call me Sam. That's my message. Pretentiousness reveals that you aren't comfortable in your own skin. It also violates our casual Pacific Northwest lifestyle and sense of egalitarianism. We're public servants—not royalty.

Just as it's important not to take yourself too seriously, it is essential not to take the political give-and-take personally. If you can't keep the perspective that the brickbats and criticisms are merely a by-product of others playing their parts in the political game and you let your feelings be hurt, you shouldn't be in politics. You won't be able to sleep at night, your stomach will churn, and you will become bitter. There's nothing more pathetic in politics than seeing good people get upset over the usual banter and start plotting vendettas to get even.

Don't dwell on your mistakes, misfortunes or failures. In fact, those situations should be viewed as learning opportunities. When you slip or stumble, take stock and move forward with new insight and knowledge. Negative attitudes and pessimism bring down you, your staff and your supporters. On the other hand, perpetual optimism is a force multiplier.

If you want to accomplish anything of consequence, don't expect everybody to love you. If you are championing new policy directions or substantial change, some people are going to be upset with you, regardless of how civil and inclusive you strive to be. That's human nature. Shake off criticism and second-guessing and move forward! The end results are worth it.

In politics, it's a serious mistake to not make the time and effort to learn the craft. That's like becoming a banker without learning the banking business. Do not expect to be effective and successful without understanding how the system works and the fundamental qualities and approaches needed to succeed.

3

ON A MISSION:

If you're too busy to laugh, you're too busy.

"The Thurston County Auditor's Office is an inspired team recognized for its exceptional customer service. We strive to be innovative and exceed expectations. We treat everyone with trust and respect. Our people are the key to our success, and we create opportunities for them to achieve their best."

YOU SHOULD HAVE SEEN MY FACE when my staff plopped that mission statement in front of me. They nailed it! I enthusiastically approved. It succinctly states my personal convictions about the focus of a government agency's staff. Throughout my years of public service, I enjoyed the reputation of having exceptional staffs. Not only did we become state and national leaders, we had fun doing it. I have been fortunate to recruit and retain bright, articulate and talented people. You are probably wondering how I managed to pull that off. Keep reading.

I learned that you need to express the "big picture" purpose of their work. It's too easy to get caught up in the day-to-day grind, in which employees keep their heads down and do only what they are told. I believe in focusing on what the team is trying to accomplish. There are a couple obvious examples in the Secretary of State's Office. In Elections, the purpose is not to simply crank out a voters' pamphlet or check the signatures on proposed initiatives. The Elections staff is the guardian of democracy for the citizens of Washington. In Archives, the purpose is not to merely sort, index and store documents. We're preserving history and making it available. It is, after all, the people's history, the documents of democracy. In other words, we need to provide context.

I've always generated pride in being the best—in the state, in the Northwest, in the country. I make it a point to emphasize that we are leaders in our field. I want our staff to strive to be the best. By doing that, they transform something strong into something superb. This sense of purpose and pride means that nothing less than being an "inspired team" striving to "be innovative and exceed expectations" will do, even when draconian budget cuts increase the challenge. I've agonized over staff cuts, especially in the early 1980s and during the past four years, but I've marveled at the positive way my teams responded. Hard times call for more creativity. In my offices, creativity meant recruiting volunteers, undertaking private fundraising, using unpaid college interns (receiving college credit), setting tough-minded priorities, and seriously re-engineering our operations.

Dedicated volunteers can be game-changers. We have 165 helping us scan and index historical documents for the State Digital Archives. They are terrific people from all walks of life. Many are genealogists, and are extraordinarily conscientious about their work. They know how important it is to correctly enter dates and names. Plus, they're fun. What do they get for this? We give them one free lunch a year, and I present them with a certificate of appreciation bearing the gold State Seal. More importantly, they get the deep satisfaction of preserving history and making it accessible worldwide. We have one staff person responsible for the care and feeding of these volunteers.

She just may be the nicest person on my entire staff. She excels in expressing heartfelt appreciation, and that's just what's needed to retain volunteers.

With those wonderful volunteers, bright young interns, prioritization and re-engineering, we've continued to succeed, not only in fulfilling our mission, but also in producing nationally recognized innovations.

My personal mission statement as a leader is to recruit, inspire and retain the best people. There's no magic involved. If you want to be the best organization, you need to get the best people. If they are bright and capable with a good work ethic, they can be trained for most positions. A remarkable example is Val Wood Handfield. As an unwed mother at the age of 15, she had to drop out of high school. We hired her for a "gofer" position in the Thurston County Auditor's Office. In spite of her lack of education and her background of adversity, it was obvious to me that she had tremendous potential. I loved her enthusiasm, her drive and her smarts. After promoting her to a payroll job, I took the controversial risk of plucking her out of the ranks to serve in management with responsibility for my archaic records section. I walked her into the records room, pointed to 143 years of paper records and explained that her mission was to make them electronically retrievable. I also told her to somehow, some way, come up with a new, innovative way of electronically recording formal documents (property records, marriage licenses and such). She took that records operation from the 19th century to the 21st century in two years. Her leadership ability blossomed as she inspired and energized a staff that had been used to doing things a certain way because "that's the way we've always done it." She became a national expert in this field. Plus—and now we're getting into important matters—Val led our office's co-ed softball team, the Aud-Balls, in home runs.

I've learned that you give people like Val an important job and get out of their way. Let them know you believe in them. Work with them to come up with clear goals—goals that stretch them. Don't micromanage. Don't become a prisoner of process. You cannot hold people responsible for results if you control the methods. Delegate responsibility, not work. Assign complete projects, not tasks. It's also crucial to give people the tools they need to do the job via training, equipment and support.

Hiring the right people is critical. In every position I've held—including Secretary of State—I've made a major time commitment to interview each employee before he or she is hired. I want a one-on-one conversation so I can judge whether this person will meet my standards and expectations. For starters, I look them in the eyes and inquire: "Why do you want this job?" If their response is, in essence, "I need a job," that's the wrong answer. We had a fellow apply to produce publications for the Elections Division. When I asked if he cared about elections, his response was essentially "no." He was interested in publications. I concluded that he was the wrong person for the position—and he was. Staff members must want to make a difference—to believe in the purpose of the position.

It is essential to be flexible and creative to retain exceptional staff members. This involves such important considerations as supporting new leadership opportunities in the office (both official and volunteer activities); opportunities for more training, including continuing professional education; and active involvement in governmental and professional associations. It also includes giving people encouragement and flexibility to provide community leadership; more money; and appropriate recognition for significant accomplishments.

It is essential to continue to keep exceptional staff members fresh and engaged. As Thurston County Auditor, I had a terrific team of managers whose accomplishments won several state and national awards. In 1993, however, I noticed they were getting stale. I decided to shake them up by making a drastic change: I rotated each manager to a different section. That was a little crazy, but it worked. The initial reaction was tantamount to shock, from both managers and the people they managed. But it succeeded in transforming the situation, exposing a serious problem and, in the end, making it possible for us to move to a higher level of performance.

Whether you're managing a public office, a private business or a group of volunteers, nothing is more fundamental than recruiting, inspiring and retaining the best people. The next challenge is getting people with individual talents to work together as a dynamic team.

"Most of us at one time or another has been part of a great 'team,' a group of people who functioned together in an extraordinary way—who trusted one

*another, who complemented each other's strengths
and compensated for each other's limitations, who had
common goals that were larger than individual goals,
and who produced extraordinary results."*

—Peter Senge

Throughout my life, I have always enjoyed the dynamics of successful teams, whether in sports, in volunteer activities, in social groups, in political campaigns or, very importantly, in offices. I like the camaraderie, the interaction with team members, and the feeling of working together to accomplish something. Throughout my career, I have focused on building such teams in my offices and volunteer activities. I believe in that 1970s' term "synergy," which means the whole is greater than the separate parts.

My cornerstone for team-building is regular meetings. Many people *hate* meetings. I don't. What they really hate is *bad* meetings that drone on with no clear purpose. I view good meetings as essential. My leadership style has been characterized by weekly meetings of key staff members. They serve many purposes: planning together for the week (which promotes ownership); getting everyone on the same page in terms of response to critical issues; developing strategies about up-coming events or presentations; even socializing. While not on a weekly basis, I've done the same for campaign steering committees, volunteer groups and fellow elected officials—the County Auditors Association's legislative committee, for in-stance. To succeed, meetings must be productive, informative, well-organized and fun.

I also believe in the value of retreats—of getting everyone out of their offices to do goal-setting, team-building, train-ing, getting to know one another better and, very important, having fun. This doesn't have to be an expensive proposition. Going to somebody's home and having a potluck lunch works just fine. With proper, focused leadership, retreats can be transformative.

While the sense of teamwork is created with office work, it is supplemented and expanded by community involvement. My offices have fielded 24-hour teams in the American Cancer Society's Relay for Life. We've spent days working together for the United Way's Day of Caring. We've held many fun events, including talent shows and theme parties for the Combined Fund Drive. Events like these have been remarkably effective ways of getting to know one another better, to enjoying giving back to the community together, and to developing leadership skills.

My offices have the well-earned reputation of having great fun. When I was County Auditor, creative, witty staff members performed songs and dances for birthdays, baby showers, wedding showers and so forth. The Secretary of State's Office seems to have a bumper crop of people who enjoy watching their cohorts demonstrate their talents—from tap dancing to air guitar. We've had talent shows and skits at office gatherings, division potlucks, barbecues and breakfasts. Both staffs have had elaborate Halloween decorations and thematic costumes. (I was a "lame duck," complete with a crutch, in my last hurrah Halloween.)

Speaking of fun, all my offices had softball teams, the Aud-Balls and the Seals, with entertaining gatherings after the games and hilarious game reports consisting of clever parodies of a newspaper report. And we didn't just play softball. At my last two offices, we've had a jogging group during the noon hours. In the auditor's office, an energetic, athletic young woman led us in rigorous aerobics after work. When I was Assistant Secretary of State, we had a tennis tournament. We've played volleyball. We encourage weight loss via an ongoing contest and tips. I actively supported smoking cessation. In the Secretary of State's Office, we have a walking group during noon hours, as well as monthly "Walks with the Secretary," inviting the whole staff to join in.

Throughout all this, I have sung and danced, worn costumes, played softball, ran, walked and generally had a great time with my staff. Believe it or not, I've been Sonny with Cher, Dan Ackroyd in a Blues Brothers routine and—I still can't believe it—Super Elvis arriving for an employee appreciation event hanging out of a helicopter. There are those who sniffed that this was inappropriate, unprofessional and beneath the dignity of the office. To that, I say "*Baloney!*" I view these activities as vital to the *espirit d' corps* and morale of the staff. In fact, while this may sound frivolous and even silly, it is one of the keys to my success in terms of welding staffs together as dynamic, productive teams.

In both the Courthouse and the Capitol, people from other offices often commented that they wish they worked in an office like mine. I view that as a high compliment.

Throughout the years, I've noted that exceptional staffs laugh, joke and have fun together. When I became Thurston County Auditor, I couldn't believe how the staff members kept their heads down, averted their eyes and were eerily quiet. After a week of that, I posted a big sign on the wall: "IF YOU'RE TOO BUSY TO LAUGH...YOU'RE TOO BUSY!" They got the point. People rarely succeed at anything unless they enjoy doing it. Research shows that people who have fun at work reduce stress, increase the sense of team, improve customer service and feel better about coming to work in the morning.

That doesn't mean that all workdays are fun. There are times when you have to grind out the work or meet a tough deadline. But overall, I take pride in my former staff members telling me that they never enjoyed a job as much before or after working for me. That means a lot to me.

Strive to Be Innovative. Nothing excites most staff members more than knowing that their work is on the cutting edge of their profession. It sure gets my adrenalin going. That means being willing to take risks. Let people make mistakes. That means taking responsibility. A leader cannot distance himself or herself from the staff at the first sign of trouble. Defend them. Protect them. Go to bat for them.

Here's how you set up an organizational culture of innovation: Constantly reorganize, be nimble, have flexible structures. When employees start in a new position, challenge them to question everything and to come up with a way of doing the job that is more efficient and provides better customer service. For an organization to remain effective, it must continually challenge itself.

With apologies to David Letterman, here is my Top 10 list of phrases that really irritate me:

10. That's not my job!
9. That would be breaking the rules.
8. It isn't in the budget.
7. It's too much work.
6. Let's form a committee and study it first.
5. We shouldn't rock the boat.
4. Everybody likes things the way they are now.
3. We don't have the time.
2. If we do that, some people are going to get upset.

... and the Number One phrase that *really* irritates me
(drum roll, please):

We've always done it that way.

To avoid these negative obstacles to innovation, I used staff retreats focused on team-building, sharing ownership and upbeat brainstorming. I also used speakers who challenged the staff to think outside the box, films featuring national advocates of innovation and information regarding the latest management theories. I always selected key staff people to lead the change. This doesn't mean that we move blindly ahead with innovations; rather, it means you need some fearlessness and willingness to accept that some people will be uncomfortable or unhappy with you. That is the price of being a leader.

Another successful approach I've used through the years is swiping good ideas. I have no shame about this. When I became County Auditor, the first thing I did was send staff members to other counties to see what they were doing better than Thurston County. Why rediscover the wheel? We went to national conferences to steal good ideas from leading counties around the country. Some ideas took years to implement. Some involved organizing the County Auditors Association's legislative committee to work with me to change laws that blocked or restrained innovations. For example, I teamed up with the manager of records and elections in King County to organize a major election conference in 1985. The goal was to dramatically reconceptualize our state's elections processes and the role of county election offices for the 21st century by showcasing changes being made in other parts of the country and brainstorming innovative ideas for the future. Staff members played a major role in the conference.

By the same token, we always have been the first to step up and share our offices' innovations with others. I take pride in having our ideas swiped.

Major innovations are not easily accomplished. Success requires thoughtful strategies and tactics. One of the best examples I've ever been involved with is the Washington State Digital Archives—a worldwide benchmark of innovation. During the 2001 legislative session, when I first advocated this ambitious program to digitize public records, many observers viewed it as a flight of fancy, a pipe dream. Most archivists—including those in my own office!—did not buy into the concept. They were locked into paper or film. Period. Most legislators didn't get it, either. They thought that "digital" and "archives" were contradictory. Since colleges and correctional institutions were aggressively competing for the state's bond money for construction projects, political realists said there was no way we'd get the money to construct a new building.

In spite of all this, we succeeded. The Washington State Digital Archives was built and recently topped 110 million documents scanned. Visitors are coming to Cheney, Wash., from China, Great Britain, Singapore and Australia, as well as from all over the United States to learn how we are doing this.

We succeeded by coming up with innovative financing—using a Certificate of Participation funded by fees. We rallied stakeholders from local government to join forces with us. I arranged with the president of Eastern Washington University to host the facility on his campus. Assistant Secretary of State Steve Excell brought legal knowledge, construction knowledge and passion to the project. I was fortunate to hire the national dean of State Archivists, Jerry Handfield, to provide professional knowledge and leadership. He also is a consummate cheerleader. The Microsoft Corporation has been an outstanding private-sector partner. The innovation has been a huge success. The office staff takes great pride in being the leader in the nation, and possibly the world, in digital archiving.

Having succeeded in such a daring, path-breaking innovation, other divisions of the office have not hesitated to be the first state in the nation to have online candidate filing and the second to have online voter registration. We boast one of the best online corporation-filing systems in the country, and we're a leader among the country's state libraries in digitizing records and publications.

Throughout my years of public service, I have pushed my staffs to be on the cutting edge of change. As County Auditor, I received eight national achievement awards for innovation. As Secretary of State, I received several national awards as well. I didn't do it alone. We lived up to the mission statement through teamwork. It is exciting. It is challenging. It makes history. Best of all, it serves the people well. It changes the way they experience government.

While leaders always focus on their staff's responsibility to them, they don't give nearly enough thought to their responsibility to the staff. Build a climate of trust, mutual loyalty and openness. Show up on time. Start meetings on time. Be considerate of their work and their obligations.

Never abuse your staff. They have lives outside of work. And this is very important: Don't take their dignity by criticizing them in front of others.

Let them know how they are doing. For those who are doing well, be sure to tell them. Be specific. Don't give syrupy, vague speeches. They don't mean anything. Know what he or she did and recognize it specifically. Celebrate small wins. Over the years, I've observed that it is way too easy to not say anything when staff members are doing well. Speak up.

However, when performance is unacceptable, you must act. It's too easy to avoid that and give misleading performance evaluations because you don't want to hurt someone's feelings. That's a recipe for trouble, maybe even expensive trouble. Discipline poor work. Fire people when necessary. It may sound counterintuitive, but this is necessary for staff morale. If someone isn't carrying his or her load or is a serious problem, it creates resentment and impacts the motivation of others. Avoiding taking action also is a disservice to someone who is failing. That person needs to find a job that fits his or her capabilities.

I find mentoring and encouraging growth to be the most rewarding part of leadership. It is particularly rewarding to spot potential and provide the encouragement and support to see that potential flower. Public service provides extensive opportunities for mentoring.

Finally, communicate, communicate, communicate. Timely chats, notes and staff meetings work. Rudy Giuliani said it well: "Employees should not have to divine their boss's ideas and preferences." I have found this to be a challenge for me, but it is one of the most important responsibilities to one's staff members.

When a government employee or a volunteer is doing well, there is usually no way to reward them monetarily. Thus, it is important to recognize them and thank them in other ways. This is a wonderful opportunity to be creative. Over the years, we've done it with my staffs through employee recognition events, plaques, certificates and personal notes. But the most valuable recognition comes from personal comments. In the County Auditor's Office, we had customer service cards. Rather than having check marks for performance, the cards read, "Did Someone Do Something Special?" Customers loved to fill them out when they were treated well. Staff members coveted them—often lining their walls with them. Each time we received one (which was often), I personally thanked the staff member. That seemingly small, inexpensive recognition inspired staff members to go the extra mile for customers.

One of the fundamental duties of the leader or manager is to recognize and reward. Two of the most powerful words in the English language are "thank you."

So let me say this to you: "Thank you!" What an honor and

a privilege it has been to work with so many remarkable staff members during the last 45 years. I've thoroughly enjoyed our successes, our exciting times, even our tough times—and what each of them has meant to me personally. They are the main reason I've loved my job throughout my career.

4

POLITICAL LIFE:

Flourish in the Hothouse of Politics.

*"This is my life, it is my stewardship,
and I am responsible and accountable for it."*

—Stephen Casey

EVERY MONTH SEEMS TO BE pockmarked by stories about elected officials whose lives have been destroyed by alcohol or drug addiction, sex scandals, corruption, bizarre behavior or shocking inattention to critical aspects of the jobs the people elected them to do. Some just get so caught up in the perks of their positions that they lose sight of the public trust.

During my years of public service, I've seen sad, self-destructive behavior by otherwise talented, decent people. Happily, they represent a distinct minority of the officeholders I've known. The cautionary tale for us all, however, is that good people can lose their way under pressure if their lives lack balance. One of the biggest challenges in public life is how to avoid allowing politics and the stress of an overflowing in-basket to overshadow marriage, family, friends, mental and physical health, and staying involved in one's community. I'm reminded of a campaign manager who missed the birth of his daughter because it interfered with a debate. The candidate should have sent him where he belonged—the hospital.

The problem starts with the bad reasons why some people run for public office—glory, power, prestige, a pension or a stepping stone to run for something else, among them. To thrive in the fish bowl of public office, you must believe you can make a difference. It's not just another job. It has to make you come alive. It should be your mission in life.

I went on College Civics Tours around the state every spring. Inevitably, the first question students asked was why I chose to be a public official. My answer has never varied over the years: No matter what field you're in—from computer programming to wine-making—success is doing what you find fulfilling. I told them I found my niche early on. I could have done a lot of other things and made a lot more money, but for me, the rewards of public service are more than monetary. I told them it's not just making a living that's important. Whether it's the hectic life of a single mom, a student with two jobs and three loans, a business executive or an elected official, leading a balanced life presents the same basic challenge. Yet nothing is more important in the long run.

It all starts with marriage and family. A deep commitment of time, effort and focus needs to be present. Loved ones are the anchor that keeps you down to earth—the unconditional love that is essential in anybody's life. I know it's hard, but it's important to block out definitive time for the people you care about. I'm talking about real vacations with no e-mails, Facebook or iPhones. It can be done. Trust me. When he was governor, Gary Locke had young children. He had his staff block out weekends—and it usually worked. Whenever I visited the Governor's Mansion and saw a tricycle on the porch, it made me smile. The Lieutenant Governor and I had to fill in for him regularly, but I didn't mind. I admired and respected his commitment. For me, there is nothing as special as spending a sunny afternoon at Lake Wenatchee playing on an isolated sandy beach with my grandsons. We make castles, dig canals, build forts, swim, splash, row and lollygag the day away. Nothing else in life can compare with those memories. And those moments are fleeting. If you miss them, you can't get them back.

It also is important to make time for friends. Longtime friendships sustain you through the good times and tougher times. In my case, it helps to have some non-political friends who care more about tennis or bridge than about the body politic. As with family, it takes a commitment of time and effort to maintain those friendships.

But if you lack the energy to walk on the beach or toss a baseball with your sons; if you can't sleep at night because your back aches or your blood pressure is off the charts, you're in trouble. You have forgotten to take care of yourself. We all need physical exercise and proper nutrition. It helps if it is fun. Throughout the years, I've gone on runs and played ball with staff members. It was good for all of us and built camaraderie. I've been going to weight-lifting training with my wife. We both enjoy it. Regular physical exercise is one of the cheapest, most effective ways to relieve stress, live longer and stay sharper. In other words, it is an essential part of doing well in any profession. Unfortunately, it is way too easy to take on additional professional obligations and demands. (Tell me about it!) But to lead a balanced life, you have to learn to prioritize family and take care of yourself.

OK, you may take good care of yourself and still run out of gas. After doing the same job for years, you can become stale. It is too easy to sink into a rut; to become territorial; to just go through the motions. In any profession with high demands and stress, burn-out is not only possible, it is probable. My antidote for burn-out is to search out challenging opportunities to change, grow, innovate and improve. There's a need to stay fresh. You can't just talk yourself into it. You have to do something about it. I have found a number of ways to recharge my batteries. One is to learn and improve continuously. I read a lot, especially biographies of major political figures. It's hard to imagine anything more stressful for a politician than presiding over a Civil War. Lincoln created "a team of rivals." What an inspiring, instructive story.

Or consider what Lewis and Clark faced with "undaunted courage" when Jefferson gave them the assignment of a lifetime. These are thought-provoking stories that provide historical perspective and offer insight into how to provide effective leadership.

I also have found it renewing to attend conferences, symposia and forums. I find myself taking copious notes, including a separate list of "new ideas" to work on when I get back to the office. Volunteer leadership is another way to jump-start yourself out of a rut. Getting out of the office and into a different situation is refreshing and an opportunity to learn new leadership skills.

If you can't get enthusiastic about your work, it is imperative to take action to switch gears. However, enthusiasm isn't enough. You also need to be committed to taking care of the details. If you are going to sign a public document, approve a campaign flier or put your signature on your campaign's financial disclosure report, it's your reputation that is on the line. I particularly encourage you to be cautious when a campaign manager or consultant wants you to sign off on negative advertising about your opponent. That campaign staffer can walk away untainted. You have to live with it and, often, with your opponent. It's your reputation. By taking a few minutes to consider the long-run consequences and to review the fine print, you can save yourself some major embarrassment or even a costly lawsuit. Since this is a state with strong open public records laws, any document, e-mail or social media item can end up on the front page of the newspaper or blasted through cyberspace.

I can't stress enough how important it is to realize that as a public official, you are making history. You have a momentous personal responsibility to preserve that history for future generations. Have a good filing system. Be well organized in preserving your records. As you prepare to leave public office, have your records properly organized and shipped to the Washington State Archives. The staff there will carefully index and store the records and will make them available for researchers.

Details that can't be delegated are returning phone calls, responding in a timely fashion to electronic and written correspondence and showing up on time for meetings and public appearances. Be there when you said you would. Be a person who can be trusted. Otherwise, you display arrogance. People will think you are a jerk—or at best, disorganized.

One of the challenges of public office is the unpredictability that comes with each day. Sometimes your priorities change every time the phone rings. Being constantly interrupted with calls, e-mails and visitors, it is up to you to keep track of important goals by keeping a to-do list. It's the key to staying focused on priorities and thereby controlling your time.

One of the important priorities for a public official is giving time and talent on behalf of community causes. You may be the busiest person in your community, but your community still needs you. It's all right to lend your name to a cause, but you also need to be visible and to give substantive support. The same skills you use to get elected and to serve successfully can be tremendously valuable for a community cause. Successful politicians tend to be good organizers, good networkers and good communicators. They are good at raising money. Those skills can take a struggling group and make it successful. Getting involved in charities or nonprofits also provides you with growth opportunities as a leader. Recruiting, organizing, inspiring and retaining volunteers are great training for managing public employees. You learn or refine skills that can make a big difference in your career. Moreover, you are extending your network by being active in your community. If you are willing to step up and help community activists, they likely will be there for you when you need help.

I've found that those of us who are attracted to public service find giving back to the community very fulfilling. If you are able to make a significant difference for a community project, you are accomplishing something beyond the scope of your office.

These things are what I've learned in my public service career. If you follow my advice, I think you'll have a roadmap on how to avoid becoming one of those self-destructive politicians in the headlines and, instead, flourish in the hothouse of politics. Again, to be successful, an officeholder needs a clear sense of purpose and a balanced life. Family and health matter enormously. Avoid burnout. Don't get stuck in a rut. Don't forget or ignore important details. Give back to the community.

Politics is a noble calling. It's also satisfying—and fun, if you keep things in perspective.

Looking Forward

I CONCLUDE MY LONG CAREER with much optimism for the future of Washington state politics. I'm impressed by the new crop of legislators and local officials. I like their civility, their moderation and their pragmatic approach to the political process. This is the case on both sides of the aisle.

During the last two legislative sessions, I held Wednesday morning breakfast discussions with most of the freshmen and sophomore Republican legislators. They couldn't have been more receptive to exploring ideas bigger and more visionary than narrow partisan politics.

During the past seven years, at college campuses around our state, I've talked with students about their responsibility to be active in the political process and to give back to their communities. There's a generational tendency to question whether the "kids" have the requisite zeal to pick up the torch. I've been struck by the deep commitment these college students have to give of themselves, their time and their talents to help their communities and their country.

People of both parties have been lamenting my departure. They say I may be the "last of a breed." In a way, I'm flattered. But they are wrong. We have some exciting, bright, capable young leaders coming up. I've met them, talked with them and been inspired by them.

As old politicians like to say, it has been "a distinct honor and privilege" to serve the people of the great state of Washington. Those aren't just words. When I say it, I really mean it.

It is definitely you, the people, that I will miss the most. I owe a special debt of gratitude to all the staff members who have helped me succeed over the years—and to my fellow elected officials, from the Courthouse to the Capitol, who have greatly enriched my life and career. They are the key to any successes I enjoyed.

I leave with the hope that this little handbook is of some help to future political generations. It is from the heart.

—Sam Reed
Olympia, Washington
December, 2012

Wedding, August 11, 1963

Governor/Secretary of State softball team 1969

Doorbelling for State Representative Dan Evans campaign for Governor, Summer 1964

LC Class of '58 Picks Lead...

LEWIS and Clark high school class of 1958 heads into its final four months of activities with new officers. Outgoing president Jack Malone (left) congratulates Sam Reed, president. Others (from left) are Gretchen Swanson, secretary; Paul Barton, fifth executive; Sandra Dyke, vice leader, and Gary Cromer, treasurer.

Elected Lewis and Clark High School's senior class president, January 1958

Thurston County Auditor's softball team, the Aud-balls, summer 1984

Governor Dan Evans announcing Sam's appointment to be the Director
of the Governor's Urban Affairs Council, June 1967

Campaigning in the fall of 2000

Speaking at an event at Seattle's Roosevelt High School urging
18-year-old students to register and vote

Combined Fund Drive kickoff event, a tricycle race

Greeting students at Franklin High School in 2003

Shirt says, "I can only please one person each day. Today is not your day" with Alex Galvez

Press conference in December 2004

Grandsons visit the office

Leading the "survivors lap" for the relay for life

With staff at Public Service recognition week, Stephanie Horn (l) and Dawn Sanquist (r).

Playing with grandsons at Lake Wenatchee

Performing "Blues Brothers" talent show act at the 2009
Combined Fund Drive kickoff event with Brian Zylstra

Story time at a local library

Baby kissing on the campaign trail in 2008

Awards presentation at an office employee appreciation event